Executive Compensation for Private Company CEOs and Business Owners

Quick and Easy Tips to Help You Manage Your Largest Investment

Larry Comp

Steve Smith

LTCperformance
strategies

Executive Compensation for Private Company CEOs and Business Owners

Copyright © 2014 LTC Performance Strategies, Inc.

All rights reserved. No part of this book may be reproduced or transmitted in any form or by any means, electronic or mechanical, including photocopying, recording, or by any information storage and retrieval system, without the written permission of the Publisher, except where permitted by law.

Published by
LTC Performance Strategies, Inc.
28001 Smyth Drive
Suite 103
Valencia, CA 91355
www.ltcperformance.com

Manufactured in the United States of America, or in the United Kingdom when distributed elsewhere.

Comp, Larry and Smith, Steve

Executive Compensation for Private Company CEOs and Business Owners: Quick and Easy Tips to Help You Manage Your Largest Investment

   Worthy Shorts ID: RSP127

ISBN:	978-1-937506-69-8	Paperback
	978-1-937506-70-4	eBook

Warning- Disclaimer

The purpose of the book is to educate and guide. The authors or publisher does not guarantee that anyone following the techniques, suggestions, tips, ideas, or strategies will be successful. The author and publisher shall have neither liability or responsibility to anyone with respect to any loss or damage caused, or alleged to be caused, directly or indirectly by the information contained in this book.

Giving Back

In keeping with LTC Performance Strategies' values, a percentage of the proceeds from sales of this book will be donated to our favorite charity: Family Promise of Santa Clarita Valley.

About Family Promise of Santa Clarita Valley

Family Promise of Santa Clarita Valley is a non-profit (501c3) public benefit organization that began operations in Santa Clarita in June of 2011 to serve homeless children and their families. Family Promise of SCV is one of over 180 affiliates across the country of Family Promise, a national nonprofit organization committed to helping low-income families achieve lasting independence. (www.familypromise.org)

Family Promise of SCV partners with over 23 local congregations of different faiths in the Santa Clarita Valley to provide overnight lodging, meals and hospitality for homeless children and their families on a 24/7, 365 basis. One of the unique aspects of Family Promise is a dedicated focus on identifying and solving the underlying causes of homelessness.

Comprehensive support services are provided to the adult family members. Each one receives intense personal and career counseling that includes the development of a plan tailored to the specific needs of their family. This has resulted in a nearly 80% success rate in moving families back into apartments or transitional housing, so that they can return to being stable and functioning members of the community. Through Family Promise, in a few short years, dozens of local families have been able to regain and sustain their housing, independence, and dignity.

Family Promise of SCV is predominantly funded via generous donations, grants, gifts, and volunteer services provided by local businesses, foundations, the faith community, and citizens at large. Ongoing support, including donations and volunteer service, is required for Family Promise of SCV to continue to serve the families who desperately need help.

For more information or to make a donation visit: http://www.familypromiseSCV.org/

For Terry, my love and life partner.

*For Colin and Conner,
our greatest joy in this world.*

—Larry Comp

Acknowledgements

We'd like to take a moment to thank some wonderful folks who helped us along the way in completing our 1st Executive Compensation book: Paul Falcone, Craig Duswalt, Marc Emmer and Dana Borowka for their book writing and publishing tips; chief executives and long-term clients, Fred Ketcho and Mike Stark; Board of Advisors, Don Matso and Ravi Patel; Executive Benefits Guru, Bob Nienaber; Mastermind Partners, Fleming Jones, JoAnne Smith and Jeff Yoos; Executive Compensation Attorney, Marla Aspinwall; the many Vistage Chairs/leaders who have entrusted their clients with us, including Gary Brennglass, Jed Daly, Steve Elson, Yolanda Guibert, Bill Hawfield, Mark Hoffman, Ron Means, Mitch Pearlman, Don Riddell, Gail Shaper-Gordon, and George Walker, and, of course, the hundreds of clients who have allowed us to help them make an important difference in their own companies.

Contents

1. Managing Your Biggest Investment 1
2. Paying for Performance 5
3. Establishing Your Executive Compensation Philosophy 11
4. Clarifying Your Roles 15
5. Paying the Right Salaries 21
6. Handling Pay Increases 29
7. Driving the Appropriate Performance and Behavior (Short-Term Incentives) 33
8. Retaining Your Top Performers (Long-Term Incentives) 43
9. Selecting and Aligning Your Performance Goals 59
10. Getting Even More from Your Incentive Plans 63
11. Managing Performance 69
12. Helping Your Executives to Build Capital for the Future 75
13. Remaining in Compliance 83
14. For Business Owners Only 87

15 What to Do Now?   91

Appendix A   Sample Philosophy and Objectives Statement   95

Appendix B   Sample Job Description   97

Appendix C   Sample Mini-Job Profiles   101

Works Cited   103

The LTC Book Series

We created this book series because CEOs and owners of small- and medium-sized private companies have unique challenges. They also lack the time, resources, and patience to get the "biggest bang for their buck" in managing their largest investment (compensation).

Most of the books you'll find on compensation are too long, too theoretical, and geared to academicians, consultants, or human resources/compensation practitioners. We realize that small- and medium-sized companies are the engines running our country and that their leaders need simple, practical information—and they need it now!

This book, and our forthcoming books, are designed to be read in about an hour or two, providing you with the tools, tips, and guidelines you need to drive your company forward.

About Larry Comp

Larry Comp serves as LTC Performance Strategies' President as well as its Practice Leader for *High Performance and Total Compensation Solutions*. Larry is a widely recognized authority in the field, having led hundreds of related initiatives with over 300 organizations across 50+ industry segments. These include the design, development, and implementation of:

- Executive Compensation Programs
- Executive Benefit Plans
- Salary Management Programs
- Sales Incentive Plans
- Company-wide Incentive Programs
- Long-Term Cash/Stock-Based Plans

Larry is passionate about aligning and leveraging pay for performance relationships to create healthy, "high-performance" companies. Client organizations frequently report increased productivity and profitability as well as improved teamwork and ownership.

Prior to joining LTC, Larry held progressively responsible leadership roles with Baxter Healthcare, Nissan, and Babcock and Wilcox. He holds a Masters Degree in Human Resources Management, has been accredited as a Senior Professional in Human Resources (SPHR), and a Certified Management Consultant (CMC). Larry also holds the following licenses: Life and Health, Series 6, and Series 63.

In addition, Larry has co-authored over 50 articles and taught undergraduate and graduate classes for several universities. He has been a member of several boards and currently serves on the Compensation Committee of a large ESOP corporation and director for a prominent financial services corporation.

About Steve Smith

Steve Smith serves as LTC Performance's Director of Client Solutions. Since joining LTC in 2009, Steve has consulted on over 100 compensation initiatives. These initiatives include the design, development, and implementation of:

- Executive Compensation Programs
  - Executive Base Pay
  - Management Incentive Plans
  - Stock and Phantom Equity Plans
  - Cash-Based Long-Term Incentive Plans
  - Executive Deferral Programs
- Sales Compensation Plans
- Company-wide Goalsharing Incentive Programs
- Salary Management Plans

Steve's passion is working closely with clients to develop solutions that allow them to utilize their total compensation program to attract and retain top caliber talent, while realizing a solid return on investment. Steve strives to ensure clients' plans achieve a strong pay for performance relationship while being externally competitive and internally equitable.

Steve holds a Masters Degree in Business Administration (MBA) from Woodbury University and a Bachelors Degree in Business Administration/Law from California State University, Northridge.

Introduction

Private company CEOs and business owners face unique challenges every day, such as:

"I need to hire a chief financial officer (CFO). What will we have to pay this person?"

"Everyone's talking about the importance of a pay for performance culture—how do we get there?"

"My Head of Sales and Marketing just asked for equity—do we really need to offer her a piece of the pie?"

"I'm thinking about selling the company—what can we do to retain our key leaders through this process?"

These are the types of questions we are frequently asked. Today's chief executives need answers, sometimes right away! More often than not, they don't know where to turn. One reason for this is that most of the more reliable compensation research data is geared toward the larger public and private companies. This makes it difficult for smaller employers to know how to establish competitive pay levels without breaking the bank.

The field of executive compensation is also dynamic and highly complex. As accounting rules, labor legislation, the global economy, and competitive practices evolve, it's beneficial for chief executives to have an independent advisor(s) who is(are) readily accessible and whom they can trust. Unfortunately, many such advisors lack the necessary depth and breadth of experience to provide customized solutions for organizations like yours. Others may be unduly expensive. As they used to say on the popular 1980s TV show, *Hill Street Blues*, "Be careful out there."

You may have a specific executive compensation problem and, if so, can immediately turn to the related chapter. However, because of the interrelatedness of the various topics covered, you may benefit from a quick read of the entire book. (The book can be read in about an hour or two, providing you with the tools, tips, insights, and guidelines you need to manage your most important investment.)

If you're starting to develop your executive compensation program from scratch, the model on the next page will provide you with a "big picture" overview of how you might get from where you are to where you want to be.

```
┌─────────────────────────────────────────────────────┐
│        Analysis of Executive Compensation Trends     │
└─────────────────────────────────────────────────────┘
                          ↓
┌─────────────────────────────────────────────────────┐
│    Formulation of Compensation Positioning Philosophy│
└─────────────────────────────────────────────────────┘
                          ↓
┌─────────────────────────────────────────────────────┐
│         Determination of Program Objectives          │
└─────────────────────────────────────────────────────┘
                          ↓
┌─────────────────────────────────────────────────────┐
│           Clarification of Executive Roles           │
└─────────────────────────────────────────────────────┘
                          ↓
┌─────────────────────────────────────────────────────┐
│      Analysis of Competitive Pay Levels & Practices  │
└─────────────────────────────────────────────────────┘
                          ↓
┌─────────────────────────────────────────────────────┐
│       Assessment of Internal Equity Considerations   │
└─────────────────────────────────────────────────────┘
                          ↓
┌─────────────────────────────────────────────────────┐
│  Determination of "Mix" of Total Compensation Components │
└─────────────────────────────────────────────────────┘
                          ↓
┌─────────────────────────────────────────────────────┐
│          Establishment of Base Salary Levels         │
└─────────────────────────────────────────────────────┘
                          ↓
┌─────────────────────────────────────────────────────┐
│        Development of Short-Term Incentive Plan      │
└─────────────────────────────────────────────────────┘
                          ↓
┌─────────────────────────────────────────────────────┐
│        Development of Long-Term Incentive Plan       │
└─────────────────────────────────────────────────────┘
                          ↓
┌─────────────────────────────────────────────────────┐
│   Review of Executive Benefit Alternatives; Evaluation of │
│        appropriate Capital Accumulation Vehicle      │
└─────────────────────────────────────────────────────┘
                          ↓
┌─────────────────────────────────────────────────────┐
│            Design of Program Communications          │
└─────────────────────────────────────────────────────┘
```

Chapter 1

Managing Your Biggest Investment

We are grateful to have had the opportunity to consult with over 300 leading organizations across industry. In asking our clients about their biggest expense, we almost always get the same response: COMPENSATION.

Until a few years ago, most companies paid less attention to managing executive compensation. However, the recent economic recession seemed to wake us all up. Today, most organizations are pretty serious about getting the "biggest bang from their buck" on their executive compensation programs.

Now that the job market has been turning around, most CEOs and business owners fear an increase in voluntary employee turnover. Since the cost of turnover isn't readily apparent on the Profit and Loss Statement, historically, it hasn't received the attention it deserves. However, when you consider the cost of replacing an executive: search fees, time spent in the recruitment/screening process, loss of knowledge, disruption to the business—it all adds up. In fact, the cost of voluntary executive turnover can easily exceed 100% of the replaced executive's salary.

Over the last several years, many chief executives and human resource officers have shifted their perspective. Instead of viewing compensation as an expense, they now consider it an investment. Please note that, while it's hard to locate specific findings that quantify compensation's return on investment (ROI), a study was conducted that produced a model contrasting the productivity of top vs. average performers. Below is an excerpt pertaining to management/professional workers:

- "Average" workers' productivity = 48% more than "Non-producers"

- "Superior" workers' productivity = 48% more than "Average"

- "Superior" workers' productivity = 96% more than "Non-producers" (Beek)

Michael Sturman conducted a second study of this nature. In his study, he evaluated the economic value added to an organization from above average, average, and below average performers. Below are the conclusions from this study:

- "Average" performers' economic value added = 11x more than "Below Average"

- "Above Average" performers' economic value added = 2x more than "Average"

- "Above Average" performers' economic value added = 21x more than "Below Average" (Sturman, 2003)

What these studies imply is that if you're not hiring top-notch performers, you are costing yourself a lot of money.

In our current era, companies have to get more done with fewer employees. This has made competition for the best and the brightest tougher and tougher. Since compensation is a primary reason why executives choose to join or leave an organization, doesn't it make sense to be sure that your compensation program helps you to attract, engage, motivate, and retain those executives who can take your company to increasingly higher levels?

Chapter 2

Paying for Performance

About 15 years ago, I (Larry) was intrigued by an article that came across my desk. It described a comprehensive study in which the prominent firm, Bain Consulting, asked CEOs across the country to: (1) think about all of the various initiatives they had undertaken to drive their companies forward, and (2) to select the one that had provided them with the greatest return on investment (ROI). As I began to skim the article, I couldn't help chuckling to myself because so many of us CEOs and business owners operate by management by magazine article (MMA). That being the case, I quickly scanned the rest of the article to discover the results of this study. Of course, the list included the typical initiatives we all tend to think about—management by objectives, customer segmentation, continuous improvement, and the like. But guess what the number one initiative cited was?— PAY FOR PERFORMANCE.

OK, as an executive compensation consultant I have to admit that I was very pleased to learn of this research finding. But I had to be honest and ask myself, would pay for performance stand the test of time—or was this just another passing fad?

Well, fast-forward 15 years and we find that this topic just continues to get hotter and hotter.

You see, in the past, pay levels were largely linked to employee tenure; annual pay raises were pegged to a cost-of-living (COL) index. Of course, these COL increases had no linkage to performance and, therefore, provided a weak return on investment.

In the past, it was also unusual for anyone but executives to qualify for annual bonuses. When bonuses were provided, these were typically discretionary. Of course, discretionary bonuses lack the potency needed to incent the desired performance and behavior.

Well, this has all changed over the last several years. Leading companies are now tying virtually all forms of compensation to performance. Merit increases are now predominantly linked to individual performance. Short-term incentive plans now cover most employees across the organization and are strongly linked to company and individual performance. Long-term incentive plans (i.e., stock options or cash-based LTIPs) are typically offered to the key strategic leaders and are primarily linked to longer-term performance measures. Today, even many of our executive benefit plans incorporate a pay for performance feature.

As companies implement effective pay for performance programs, they improve organizational alignment, employee engagement and motivation, financial performance, and the value and attractiveness of the enterprise. As you read on, you will notice that pay for performance has become a central variable in designing all elements of compensation.

Building a pay for performance culture can be very rewarding, but also quite challenging. We all remember the Law of Physics, right?—"For every action there is an equal and opposite reaction." Many people might say that they look forward to change, but in reality most people resist it. Therefore, when you set out to create a healthy, higher-performing company, you'll benefit from a strong plan and a firm commitment to holding yourself and your executive team accountable for making this goal a reality. Let's look at some tips you will want to consider.

1. **Commit to creating a positive, progressive culture.**

   People want to work in an environment where they are trusted and respected. If you give them the right tools and proper guidance, they will often pleasantly surprise you.

2. **Develop a "growth" mindset.**

   In this age of global competition and accelerated change, good is not good enough. We need to get out of our incremental thinking and take our businesses to higher levels.

3. **Focus on profitable growth.**

   Whether we realize it or not, all CEOs and business owners bring their own biases toward driving profitability. Some focus on sales and tend to see growth opportunities everywhere. Others focus on cost containment/reduction. Which is the proper orientation? You're right—the answer is BOTH.

4. **Get everyone "on the same page."**

   Most of us have probably been involved in strategic planning. You remember—you go offsite for a day or so and come back with a zillion ideas and a notebook full of charts and graphs. And yes, the notebook ends up sitting on a shelf with the information never shared with the troops. Look to reduce your plan to a page and share whatever you can with your employees so they can be part of "the game of business."

5. **Work smart: focus on the vital few.**

   Many companies have no clear-cut goals. Some have dozens and change them frequently, which ends up driving everyone nuts. Pick the 5-7 most important financial and non-financial goals that will serve as a guiding light during your plan year. Make sure everyone is aligned with these goals and going in the right direction.

6. **Build a company of business people**

   Make sure you have the right people in the right roles. Help them to understand business, especially your business. For your executives and other employees to be able to select the proper goals, they need to understand the big picture and what you see as important.

7. **Give them a stake in the outcome**

   Without building an entitlement culture, give your people an opportunity to earn good bonuses for strong organizational and individual performance. Help them to understand what they need to do to help the company, as well as themselves, to be successful.

8. **Hold each other accountable/execute**

   People are all too familiar with the "program of the month." Don't be surprised if they aren't too excited with your new initiative to create a pay-for-performance culture. They've been through other initiatives before and know that, oftentimes, things just go back to "normal," no matter how dismal that sounds. To achieve the desired results, you need to make sure that all of your managers are "on board" and are being held accountable. Remember, the biggest reason CEOs and business owners fail is that they fail to execute. Don't become another statistic.

The concept of pay-for-performance is, simply put, difficult to disagree with. This is the main reason it has been integrated into all facets of total compensation. Given the fact that compensation is generally an organization's largest investment, doesn't it make sense to design your total compensation plan in a way that gives you the biggest "bang for your buck"?

Chapter 3

Establishing Your Executive Compensation Philosophy

During the early 1990s, I (Larry) served as an HR leader with a highly respected, global medical device company. We were on a hiring spree and, like our competitors, intent on attracting the best candidates. Of course, these candidates, in turn, were looking to work for the best companies. Occasionally, one of them would ask me about our company's compensation philosophy and I would proudly state that we paid at the 75th percentile, which means that we were paying more than 75% of what the other companies within our respective market were paying.

One day it occurred to me that our employment value proposition, cited above, might not be all that unique. If fact, all of our competitors seemed to be using the same spiel. You know, "we pay at the 75th percentile." Whoa, was that even mathematically possible?

One day, it seemed like Corporate America woke up to the realization that paying salaries at the 75th percentile wasn't such a great idea. In essence, all we were doing was driving up our fixed costs. What we needed to do was contain these fixed expenses so we could allocate more of our total compensation budget to incentive pay, which is a variable expense.

So what did we all do in an effort to differentiate ourselves from the competition? Yep, you guessed it;

we all changed our positioning philosophies to, once again, follow one another. Now we all seem to be pegging our pay levels at the 50th percentile.

Of course, when we say 50th percentile, it's not quite that simple. Companies must consider each of the total compensation components (salary, short-term incentive, long-term incentive, benefits) that comprise their total compensation packages and how they intend to allocate dollar values across each of these components.

As you read further, you'll gather tips and ideas on how to structure each portion of your total compensation package. The important thing to note, right now, is that each portion of the mix represents a significant investment and should be tailored to meet your company's specific requirements.

Now, if you were to try to articulate how many of today's forward-thinking companies are positioning their compensation levels, it might look something like this: base salaries at or slightly below the 50th percentile, salaries plus target incentives at or somewhat above the 50th percentile. These companies typically *leverage* their pay-for-performance plans in order to contain fixed expenses (salaries) while offering significant variable pay incentives for superior results. This type of positioning sends a strong message that these companies are serious about their businesses and willing to pay generously for the desired results.

For the record, no one knows exactly where the 50th percentile is. It depends on many variables, such as the size and type of companies you are benchmarking your company against, as well as the particu-

Establishing Your Executive Compensation Philosophy 13

lar survey sources you are utilizing. We'd also like to suggest that you guard against oversimplification. In other words, before you lock yourself into a particular compensation positioning philosophy, ask yourself some key questions such as:

- What is our company's stage of evolution? For instance, are we a "start-up" or a mature organization?

- Are we offering a long-term compensation component or just salary and an annual incentive?

- What are we able to afford at this time?

Once you have determined your compensation positioning philosophy, we then suggest formulating a set of associated program objectives. These objectives will serve as a foundation for your executive compensation program. Your set might include objectives such as:

- Attract and retain top caliber executives

- Incent the desired organizational and individual performance

- Be externally competitive and internally equitable

- Ensure a strong pay for performance relationship

- Comply with applicable regulations

You can then step back each year to assess your executive compensation program against your stated

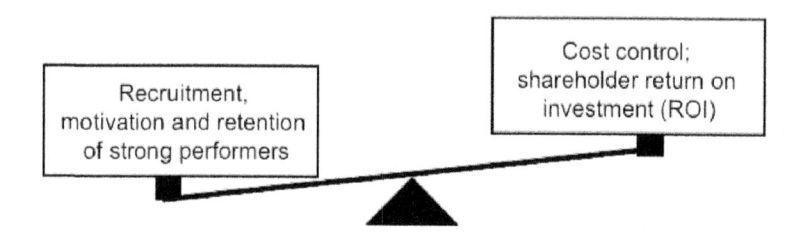

[Recruitment, motivation and retention of strong performers] ⟷ [Cost control; shareholder return on investment (ROI)]

objectives. This will allow you to see where you've been successful, as well as where any improvements may be needed in the future.

In an effort to be more helpful, we have taken the opportunity to provide you with a sample Compensation Philosophy and Objectives Statement (Appendix A).

In the meantime, the teeter-totter diagram, above, will serve as a gentle reminder that managing compensation, your company's largest investment, is no easy matter. Compensation is both an art and a science, and managing it requires a delicate balance. In essence, you need to pay enough to attract, motivate, and retain top talent while, at the same time, managing associated costs to achieve a strong return on total compensation dollars expended.

Chapter 4

Clarifying Your Roles

Despite all the testimonies we hear regarding the productivity of the U.S. workforce, our organizations are nowhere near as productive as they could be. Conservative estimates indicate that the average employee wastes as much as 25% or more of his/her time each day (Wow!). While some of this is due to not doing things right the first time, much of the problem stems from working on low priority items—or on work that no longer needs to be done.

The above paragraph may have conjured up a picture in your mind of a bunch of ineffective, lower-level, non-exempt employees. Sure, some of these individuals are not as productive as they could be, but chances are they have a pretty good idea of what they're supposed to do—and they also tend to be pretty closely supervised. But what about some of the executives you may have hired along the way. Aren't they supposed to know what to do—and what to focus on? Well sure, but they tend to have a lot more discretion in carrying out their roles, and, chances are, that you, as the CEO or business owner, may be out of sync with some of them.

A factor that often compounds this problem in small- to medium-sized private companies is that many of their executives fulfill multiple roles. For example, a financial executive who heads up IT or a human resources executive who also manages facilities and payroll. These "hybrid" roles are not nearly as common in the larger publicly-traded companies that have the size and resources to allow their executives to be more specialized. So, while it is often more efficient for smaller private companies to utilize "hybrid" roles, care must be taken to ensure that such roles and their associated responsibilities are well defined.

Try this exercise: Ask one of your executives to independently make a list of what he/she considers to be his/her key job responsibilities in order of priority. Mention that you will also be putting together the same list in terms of how you see this executive's priorities. Once you've both completed your lists, exchange them and compare your answers. Chances are, you may find that the two of you haven't been "on the same page." Of course, it's better to learn this sooner rather than later. If you've found that your executive who is earning $100,000 per year is wasting or misdirecting 20% of his/her time, you may have just saved your company $20,000. However, this figure is actually understated because it doesn't recognize the compounding effect of this problem; nor does it recognize the opportunity costs missed by focusing on some of the wrong priorities. According to a *USA Today* Report, CEO tenure has declined from 10 years to about 5.5 years since the 1990's (Petrecca & Strauss, 2012). Many of these executives have been "let go." We wonder how much of this turnover may be due to misunderstandings about roles, goals, and priorities?

Ok, so we've just focused on the importance of clarifying the executive role. However, each execu-

Clarifying Your Roles

tive's success is largely due to the collective efforts and contributions of his/her employees. Therefore, doesn't it make sense for each executive to make sure his/her employees' roles are also clear and aligned?

Thankfully, many conflicts can be avoided by clarifying roles at the time of hire. Here are some simple tools to consider in remedying related problems.

Job Descriptions

Job descriptions are generally 1-2 page documents that summarize the purpose of each role and clarify key responsibilities and position requirements. For many positions, responsibilities can be listed in order of priority or time expended. For jobs that follow a specific routine, responsibilities can be listed in chronological order.

Mini Profiles

Mini profiles are much more concise than traditional job descriptions. Both describe organizational roles and requirements, but the mini profiles do so in a much more abbreviated manner.

In the past, most of our clients opted for job descriptions. They realized that the additional detail that job descriptions provide could help them to be more effective when it came to executing key business activities such as recruitment, selection, orientation, coaching, and performance development. On the other hand, job descriptions take more time to prepare and are difficult to keep current for organizations experiencing a great deal of change and/or operating with lean Human Resources staff. For such organizations, mini profiles may prove to be the most viable tool.

Based upon your company's specific requirements, you may choose to utilize job descriptions, mini profiles, or both.

Whichever approach you decide to use to clarify your employees' roles, here are a few benefits you should realize:

- Staff members will feel more secure

- The organization will realize greater synergy

- The likelihood of related conflicts will decrease

- Productivity (and profits) will increase

- You will enjoy more positive relations with your staff

As private company executives and entrepreneurs, we often resist structure. Some of us may even see job descriptions as limiting. But here's where we may benefit from looking at the world from the perspective of our staff members. The majority of these individuals want to do a good job for us. Most come to work for more than a paycheck: many relish the opportunity to contribute to something bigger than themselves—to make a difference. This can better be accomplished when staff members have a clear understanding of what is expected of them. As leaders, we may be pleasantly surprised to see employee motivation "take off" when staff members begin feeling more confident and competent that they are performing well and, indeed, making their contribution.

We have taken the opportunity to provide you with job description and job profile templates (Appendix B and C).

Chapter 5

Paying the Right Salaries

Establishing appropriate executive salaries is a big challenge for CEOs/owners of private companies. Pay too low a salary and you'll find it quite difficult to attract and retain the type of talent necessary to drive your organization forward. However, pay too much and you'll simply be increasing your fixed expenses and cutting into your bottom line without any correlation to performance.

A typical request we receive from a client looking for assistance in coming up with an appropriate candidate salary might sound something like this:

Client: Hi Steve, my name is Fred Munoz. I'm the CEO of a company called Scott Electronics. My friend, Bill Leon, said you were able to help him navigate through some difficult compensation challenges. I was wondering if you might be able to do the same for me?

Steve: Bill's a great guy; appreciate his referral. How can I be of service, Fred?

Client: Well, my Controller, Sally Hernandez, just resigned. She's been with us for 10 years. I need to replace her ASAP, but have no idea what to pay for this position. Sally always seemed content with her salary, but informed me that she is leaving for a better offer.

Steve: I see. Can you tell me a bit about your company, Fred, so I can better understand your situation?

Client: Sure, Steve. We're a 15-year-old private company. We manufacture electronic components for the defense industry. We've been growing about 10% per year and see some "untapped" opportunity to capture a greater market share.

Steve: Thanks, Fred. How many employees do you have and what is your projected revenue for 2013?

Client: We have about 100 employees; approximately 80 at headquarters, with the rest of our folks working out of various field locations. We did about $18M in revenue and expect to break $20M this fiscal year.

Steve: Very nice, Fred. Where is your company headquartered?

Client: We're located just outside of Miami.

Steve: Thanks, Fred. In Sally's role as your Controller, was she your top financial executive?

Client: Yes.

Steve: Had you ever considered her for a CFO role?

Client: Well, no, I sort of play that role. She was more of a tactical player. You know, very good at managing the basic accounting functions and getting our reports completed on time.

Steve: Did Sally have any responsibilities outside of your Accounting Department?

Client: Oh yes, she oversaw HR and our IT functions, as well as our receptionist and some of our administrative employees.

Steve: Sounds like your managers may need to wear a lot of hats.

Client: That's right—we're all spread pretty thin.

Steve: Would you consider bringing in a CFO if you found the right person or would you prefer to keep that responsibility and bring in another Controller?

Client: Interesting question, Steve; yes, I might. That could free me up to work on some higher-level strategic priorities.

Steve: Can you tell me a little bit about any short-term incentive plans you offer?

Client: Well, quite frankly, our plan needs some work. Right now we tie any incentive payouts to performance against our annual profitability target. I also have the discretion to adjust any bonuses at the end of the year. Sally's bonus incentive target has been 15% of her salary. We've paid close to target the last few years.

Steve: Do you provide any equity or other types of long-term compensation?

Client: No, but, confidentially, we are thinking about selling the company within the next 5-7 years. I may need to offer some type of long-term incentive plan for retention purposes, as well as reward some of our key strategic leaders for driving longer-term performance and increasing the value and attractiveness of our company.

Steve: Thanks Fred, this has been very helpful. Anything else I need to know at this point?

Client: No, I think this pretty much covers it. What do you propose?

Steve: Well, Fred, based upon your parameters, we could research Controller positions for comparable companies within the Miami geographical market. We will also factor in the additional responsibilities that your controller has. If you like, we could also include survey data for a CFO position. We would provide you with benchmark reports from at least 2 reputable sources; this would include salaries at the 25th, 50th, and 75th percentiles along with the median paid short-term incentive. If you like, we could also include some information on long-term compensation practices since you are concerned about long-term retention.

Client: Sounds great, Steve. Will you be able to review these reports with me?

Steve: Of course, Fred, How about if we carve out some time tomorrow afternoon to debrief on our findings and discuss some alternative approaches to putting together a compensation package.

Client: Excellent, Steve, talk to you then.

Coming up with appropriate executive salaries, in some respects, is easier for publicly traded companies. First of all, there is a lot more competitive survey information available for these organizations. Second, public companies are now required to detail the total compensation packages of their 5 highest paid executives in their annual Proxy Statements. This information is available to the public.

Small- and medium-sized private companies are, therefore, at a disadvantage when it comes to identifying comparable pay data and developing appropriate executive compensation recommendations. However, competitive market data is available for anyone willing to purchase the information. A note of caution: the cost and quality of these surveys vary considerably.

There are 4 major variables that influence executive compensation pay levels. The first and foremost is the role. This, of course, can be fairly straightforward or, in the case of "hybrid" roles, can be somewhat complex. This is why proper role clarification is crucial prior to developing external market compensation data. The other major variables are, in order of general influence: company size, location, and industry. The graphs below, from Economic Research Institute (ERI), illustrate the affect each of these variables has on a CEO's salary (Economic Research Institute, 2013).

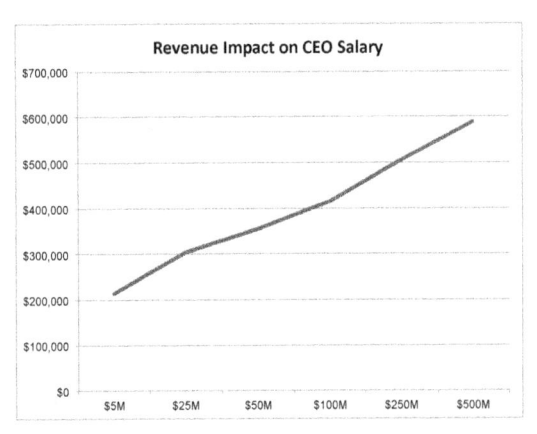

Revenue Impact on CEO Salary

Source: Economic Research Institute; All Industry Data; National (Mar. 2013)

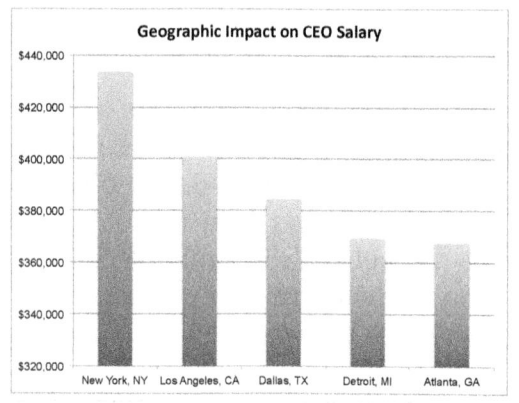

Executive Compensation

Geographic Impact on CEO Salary

(Bar chart showing approximate CEO salaries by city)
- New York, NY: ~$432,000
- Los Angeles, CA: ~$400,000
- Dallas, TX: ~$383,000
- Detroit, MI: ~$367,000
- Atlanta, GA: ~$362,000

Source: Economic Research Institute; National; $50M Revenue (Mar. 2013)

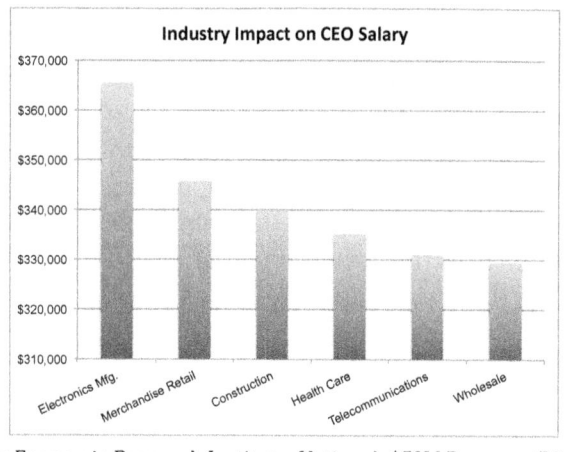

Industry Impact on CEO Salary

(Bar chart showing approximate CEO salaries by industry)
- Electronics Mfg.: ~$365,000
- Merchandise Retail: ~$345,000
- Construction: ~$340,000
- Health Care: ~$335,000
- Telecommunications: ~$330,000
- Wholesale: ~$328,000

Source: Economic Research Institute; National; $50M Revenue (Mar. 2013)

You may wish to consider purchasing a few appropriate surveys to help you assess the market competitiveness of your executive pay packages. However, more and more organizations are choosing to outsource this function rather than purchasing the reports themselves.

One reason is time. It often takes a good bit of time to get up to speed in learning how to effectively utilize many of these surveys.

A second reason is cost. Many of these surveys are fairly expensive and require annual subscriptions.

A third reason is the analysis itself. No single survey source is perfect. Sample sizes, the makeup of companies within the sample, and survey methodologies all vary from one source to the next.

A qualified executive compensation specialist can help you determine which surveys are best for evaluating your various positions and how to make sense of the various compensable factors (i.e., location, size, industry, company's stage of evolution, positioning philosophy, role, scope, incumbent/candidate experience and training, internal equity).

Chapter 6

Handling Pay Increases

A few years ago I (Steve) designed a salary administration program for a prominent global distribution client. In reviewing their salary data, I was shocked to learn that some of their hourly-paid stock clerks were earning around $50,000 per year in a very low paying area of the U.S. In essence, they were being paid about two times as much as many of the other employees in their same job classification.

When we inquired about why these individuals were paid so well, we found out that these 30+ year employees had received the "normal" pay increases every year they were employed. This practice, of course, resulted in their being significantly overpaid for their particular role. (Can you imagine the financial impact of this same practice being applied to a group of long-term executives?)

In the past, average annual executive merit increases were in the neighborhood of 8%. However, when companies began focusing on holding down fixed costs (salaries) and allocating more of the total pay "mix" to variable pay, increase percentages began to dwindle. Annual merit increases now average about 3% (Miller, 2012).

Since it appears we have gotten through the last economic recession, the job market has significantly turned around. We are now hearing more and more stories about individual job candidates who are receiving multiple job offers. With this recent turnaround in the job market, astute CEOs and business owners are now quite concerned about losing their higher-performing executives and, as such, are finding creative ways to retain them. For instance, while most U.S. companies are budgeting in the neighborhood of 3% for their merit-increase pools, some are quietly singling out their "star" performers and granting them significantly larger pay increases. (Some of these increases have been as much as 15% of annual salary.)

Given the increasing importance of "pay for performance," many companies have developed simple administrative tools, such as merit increase allocation matrices, to more intelligently and effectively allocate limited annual merit increase dollars. Such tools are built around an annual merit budget. Any merit increases are then granted based upon: (1) where employees are paid within their pay range (comp-ratio) and (2) their individual performance rating.

We developed the sample matrix below to illustrate how budgeted increase dollars could be allocated in a more efficient, objective, consistent, and cost effective manner. To calculate an employee's comp-ratio, find his/her annualized salary and the midpoint of the company's corresponding pay grade. Then divide the pay rate by the midpoint to get his/her comp-ratio (see illustration on the next page). To then find the employee's recommended pay increase, locate the appropriate comp-ratio on the vertical axis and

Merit Increase Allocation Matrix

Comp-Ratio		INCREASE PERCENTAGE			
MAX 112 - 120		0	0 - 1.0	1.5 - 2.5	3.0 - 4.0
104 - 111		0	1.0 - 2.0	2.5 - 3.5	4.0 - 5.0
MID 96 - 103	No Increase until performance improves	0	2.5 - 3.5	4.0 - 5.0	5.5 - 6.5
88 - 95		0 - 1.0	3.0 - 4.0	4.5 - 5.5	6.0 - 7.0
MIN 80 - 87		0 - 1.5	3.5 - 4.5	5.0 - 6.0	6.5 - 7.5
	- +	- +	- +	- +	- +
	Unacceptable	Needs Improvement	Effective	Highly Effective	Distinguished

move horizontally across the row to the column corresponding to the employee's appraisal rating. Note that the rating categories in this illustration include pluses (+) and minuses (-) to provide the supervisor with more flexibility and accuracy in calibrating individual employee performance.

The sample Merit Increase Allocation Matrix (above) incorporates 5 performance rating levels. Each company utilizes different performance rating descriptors. Some may utilize 5, like the sample above. Others may utilize 3 or 4. Regardless, the intent is the same—utilize the tool to: (1) link pay to performance, while keeping rising salaries in check, and (2) accelerate the movement of lower-paid, higher-performing employees.

Company executives, managers, supervisors, and other employees tend to very much like this type of merit increase tool in that it enhances the objectivity and consistency of the salary administration process.

Chapter 7

Driving the Appropriate Performance and Behavior (Short-Term Incentives)

> *"Building a visionary company requires 1% inspiration and 99% alignment."*
> —Jim Collins and Jerry Porras, *Built to Last*

As referenced in Chapter 2, about fifteen years ago Bain Consulting conducted a survey of CEOs across the country to discover which of the initiatives they had been focusing on (i.e., strategic planning, total quality management, customer segmentation, outsourcing) had delivered the best financial results. Of the 25 initiatives listed on the next page, pay-for-performance came out number one! Since that time, pay-for-performance has continued to grow in importance, especially with respect to short-term (performance of ≤1 year) incentive plans.

With competition becoming more and more intense, progressive leaders have found that short-term incentive plans, when properly designed and administered, are an organization's most potent vehicle for driving the desired performance and behavior. Below are some of the benefits reported from well-designed plans:

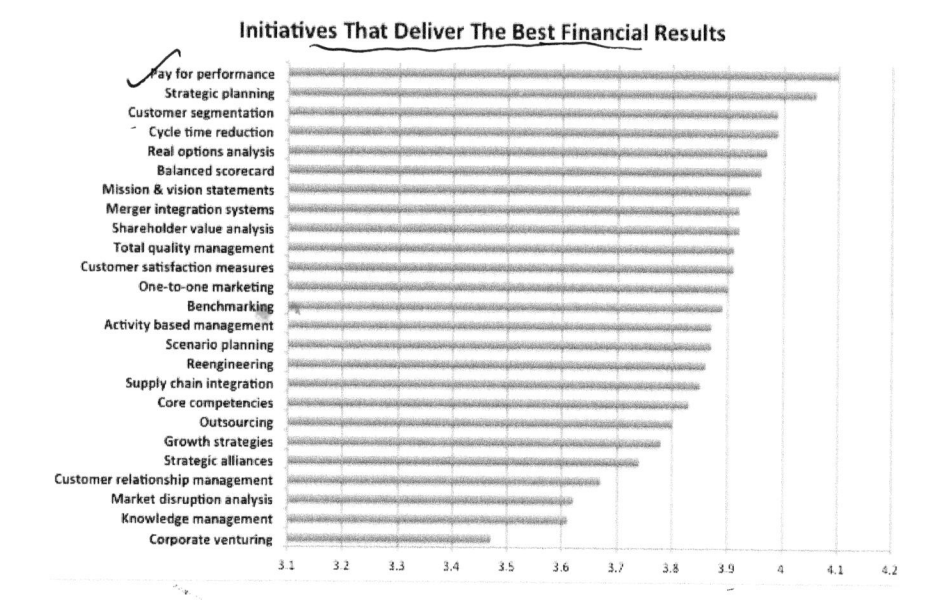

Initiatives That Deliver The Best Financial Results

Initiative	Rating
Pay for performance	~4.15
Strategic planning	~4.1
Customer segmentation	~3.75
Cycle time reduction	~3.75
Real options analysis	~3.75
Balanced scorecard	~3.75
Mission & vision statements	~3.75
Merger integration systems	~3.7
Shareholder value analysis	~3.7
Total quality management	~3.7
Customer satisfaction measures	~3.65
One-to-one marketing	~3.6
Benchmarking	~3.6
Activity based management	~3.6
Scenario planning	~3.6
Reengineering	~3.6
Supply chain integration	~3.55
Core competencies	~3.55
Outsourcing	~3.5
Growth strategies	~3.5
Strategic alliances	~3.5
Customer relationship management	~3.45
Market disruption analysis	~3.4
Knowledge management	~3.4
Corporate venturing	~3.3

- Increased revenue
- More efficient processes
- Decreased costs
- Increased skills/ knowledge
- Enhanced quality
- Improved motivation/ teamwork
- Improved customer satisfaction

The above benefits are quite compelling and probably the reason why so many companies (including almost all of our clients) offer short-term incentive opportunities to their employees.

Short-Term Incentives

For optimal results, leading companies typically "kick-off" their short-term incentive programs by focusing and aligning the executive team with a handful of critically important (annual) financial and nonfinancial goals. The success of the organization can then be largely attributed to how well the executives, as well as the employees working for these leaders, execute their responsibilities. This is why it is so important to have the right executive talent properly focused, aligned, and accountable from the start.

Each company must decide which performance measure(s) to include in their respective short-term incentive plans. While some companies may just select one measure, others may choose a dozen or so. Most of the companies we have worked with on the design of their STI plans have selected 5-7 goals. We believe that these goals, where appropriate, should include financial as well as non-financial goals and should be weighted appropriately. Of course, each company's goals may change from year to year depending on their specific circumstances. The chart on the next page, from a 2007 study, illustrates performance measurements utilized by private company participants (WorldatWork, 2007).

For several decades, we've worked closely with our clients on the design and implementation of their short-term incentive programs, and they've always experienced positive results. However, about 15 years ago, we read about a "breakthrough" goal-setting and incentive methodology called Goalsharing, which had delivered some *incredible* results. Apparently, a consultant first introduced the concept of Goalsharing to

Private Company Performance Measures

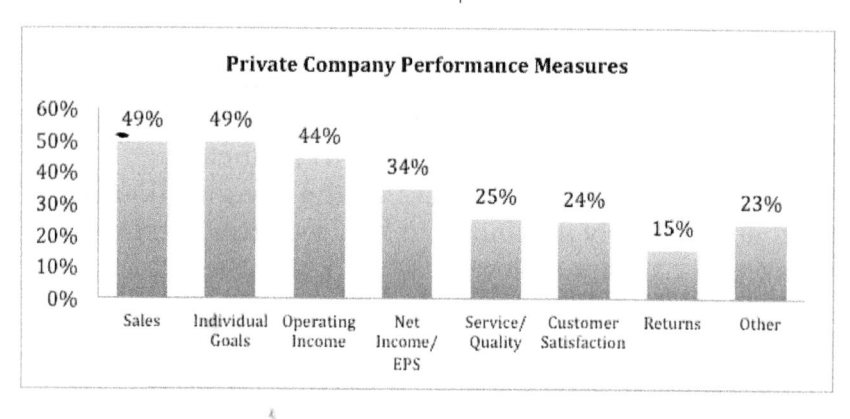

Measure	Percentage
Sales	49%
Individual Goals	49%
Operating Income	44%
Net Income/EPS	34%
Service/Quality	25%
Customer Satisfaction	24%
Returns	15%
Other	23%

Corning. Listed below are some of the extraordinary results reported by Corning's Telecommunications Product Division:

- 24x decrease in product returns,
- 10x improvement in on-time delivery,
- Awarded the coveted Malcolm Baldridge National Quality Award in 1995 (Natitional Institute of Standards & Technology, 2001).

Once we started to understand the basic tenets underlying Goalsharing, we began to examine it more thoroughly so that we could take it to higher levels with our own clients.

Let's take a few moments to look at some of the more important things we've learned about this exciting management tool. Goalsharing is not a "program of the month." It is a proven process for helping organizations to not only survive, but also to thrive in a rapidly changing, highly competitive environment.

In essence, Goalsharing is a means of working smart that engages and rewards employees for continuous improvement. Over time, it transitions employees to "business partners" and works extremely well in conjunction with business training.

Early Goalsharing pioneers recognized that employees: 1) have unique abilities, 2) prefer to understand and be involved in the business, and 3) want to make a difference. They realized that, for employees to make their contribution, they needed to understand their business and have appropriate "line of sight" —to actually see how their efforts impacted organizational results. Their organizations addressed this challenge by finding simple ways to communicate the goals of the business. They then helped staff members to see where they could make the most difference and taught them to craft simple goals that were specific, measurable, and realistic, yet had a reasonable amount of "stretch." For some, their goals may have included metrics linked to revenue generation or cost containment. Others may have focused on goal areas such as operational effectiveness/efficiency or customer satisfaction.

To improve synergy and minimize the likelihood of organizational conflict, these organizations ensured that department goals were: 1) aligned with a simple set of company financial and non-financial goals, and 2) compatible across the organization. To improve vertical alignment and employee "line-of-sight," they encouraged supervisors to provide employees with the opportunity to propose their own goals. This approach went a long way toward improving motiva-

Goal Sharing

tion and mental ownership. Participating employees were then eligible for Goalsharing incentive payments linked to company financial performance as well as individual and collective contributions against predetermined goals.

To our surprise, some of the most impressive long-term results have occurred in large, unionized companies facing difficult obstacles, such as Corning, who pioneered the concept in 1989.

Over the last decade plus, we have had the opportunity to implement Goalsharing programs with many companies across industry. Our experience has taught us that small- to large-sized clients could realize significant results quickly, as demonstrated in one of our Goalsharing case studies below:

- A small construction services company had "hit a wall." After launching one of our Goalsharing incentive programs, revenue and profit increased by more than two times, all within six months.

Our clients often ask us how long it should take before they see positive results from our Goalsharing incentive programs. We usually err on the conservative side by telling them that they can expect good results the first year, very good results the second year, and excellent results from the third year on. Of course, when they are able to experience exceptional results in 3–6 months, that's very exciting!

While larger companies typically have more resources to draw upon in implementing a Goalsharing program, we usually find that Goalsharing is easier to implement in small- to medium-sized organizations.

Short-Term Incentives

The positive results tend to come within a much shorter timeframe.

Below are some basic guidelines to help you get the biggest "bang for the buck" on your short-term incentive (Goalsharing) plans.

1. **Decide what you want to achieve from your plan(s).**

   What are your company's 5-7 most important financial and non-financial goals for the plan year? Have these goals been communicated in a way that your employees understand and appreciate? Is it clear what types of subordinate goals are needed to drive the accomplishment of your "big picture" goals? How can you get everyone aligned and going in the same direction while, at the same time, minimizing the likelihood of goal conflict?

2. **Determine the appropriate relationship between organizational and departmental/individual performance.**

   If rewards are based solely on organizational performance, what you have is a profit-sharing plan that may do little to incent your strongest performers. On the other hand, if payouts focus too much on individual/department performance, you may fall short of achieving the desired synergy to become a healthy, high-performance company. The key is reaching the right balance.

3. **Determine eligibility requirements and pertinent provisions.**

   Who will be eligible to participate in the plan? How well do these employees understand your business? Do they see a clear relationship between their efforts and the "bottom line?" Have you addressed all related plan provisions? (For instance, how employees hired during the plan year will be treated. If these employees are to be included in the plan, how will they learn about plan goals and potential rewards?) Also, how will you address employees who may be promoted, transferred, or terminated mid-course?

4. **Decide how payouts will be calculated and when these will be paid.**

   How should your short-term incentive plan fit into your total compensation strategy? How will you fund this program? What should annualized payout targets look like for each role? How should incentive payouts be linked to company and individual performance? How will you measure and reward individual contributions? What should payouts look like under divergent company and individual performance scenarios? When will you pay any earned incentives? Annually? Semi-annually? Quarterly?

5. **Decide what type of training and communications are needed to implement your program effectively.**

   Remember, a good plan, implemented well, is better than an excellent plan implemented poorly. (Of course, you will want your plan to be designed AND implemented well!)

   Research indicates that many organizations put a good bit of thought into designing their incentive plans. Unfortunately, many fall short during the "roll-out." Communication is critical here. To be effective, your managers need to understand and fully support your incentive program. They, as well as their employees, must be clear about the workings of the programs, their respective responsibilities, and what each participant must focus on to achieve the desired results.

As you can see, properly designed incentive programs can yield tremendous benefits to your company and your employees. Yet, more often than not, these plans are met with resistance. Some managers and non-management employees may resist personal accountability. Others may resist change. However, we all understand the now famous expression: "Change or Die!" Make sure you are prepared for some level of resistance and stay the course.

It is best to involve your managers and employees early in the process and to introduce these plans carefully. Since we are all creatures of habit, it is important to hold each other accountable for the success of your program. Ongoing communication is key. Some companies find it beneficial to utilize their quarterly "all-hands" meetings as an opportunity to share progress to date, celebrate successes, and "brainstorm" ideas for getting back (or staying) on track. Of course, every organization is different, so it's important to customize your program to the needs of your company. Too much is at stake here, and you do not want this to end up being just another "program of the month!"

Once you start seeing positive results, you will probably ask yourself why you didn't implement such a plan sooner!

> "A well-structured incentive program can boost productivity and instill a sense of shared responsibility among employees; a haphazardly designed program, on the other hand, can make a bad problem even worse."
>
> —Michael Alter

Chapter 8

Retaining Your Top Performers (Long-Term Incentives)

There's a wonderful global organization, called Vistage, which helps private company CEOs and business owners take their companies to the next level (www.vistage.com). Member companies of this CEO forum range from <$5 million to over $50 million in annual revenue.

These are the types of companies that are driving our country forward and Vistage members are continuously on the lookout for creative ways to gain and sustain a competitive advantage in the marketplace.

Over the last several years, we have been fortunate to work with a large number of Vistage members throughout Southern California as well as several other states. This experience has taught us a great deal about the entrepreneurial mindset as well as the challenges these executives face.

One day, we received an intriguing call from one of the local Vistage chairs. He had just finished facilitating one of his group meetings and mentioned that we would be hearing from a few of his members. The chair went on to explain that the group's meeting had focused on the controversial topic of whether or not private company owners should grant equity to their key leaders. Apparently, the discussion went back and forth and, at one point, got pretty intense. After the chair allowed the discussion to proceed for some time, he wrapped it up by suggesting that they call LTC Performance Strategies. Two members called us the next day.

By the way, the answer to the above question as to whether private companies should grant equity is: It depends. Let's look at a couple of case studies:

A few years back, we received an invitation to meet with the owner of an incredibly successful private company. We were forewarned that he was absolutely brilliant and could be quite challenging. When we met with the owner, he was everything we expected. We listened in awe as he shared his company's amazing story.

The owner's purpose in meeting with us was to better understand how executive compensation could be designed to improve executive retention. You see, the CEO, who had worked for him for several years, abruptly resigned. As the proud business owner recounted the story, we detected a degree of vulnerability as well as genuine sadness and extreme disappointment.

The owner had provided the CEO with a competitive salary and some incredibly generous annual bonuses (several million dollars during this last economic recession). Surely, the CEO would have felt eternally grateful and worked for the business owner for many, many years, wouldn't he? Well, apparently not. One day, the CEO walked into the owner's office and dropped the bomb. Apparently he had always dreamed about traveling around the world and now he had the financial resources to do so.

Long-Term Incentives

The CEO's resignation hit the owner like a ton of bricks. He was determined to never let this type of thing happen again. While the owner continues to refuse to share any equity in his company, he learned a valuable lesson about the importance of having a more intelligently designed and balanced compensation program.

Fast forward: the owner has now hired a new CEO with a very differently-structured compensation package. It consists of a reasonable salary, a much more conservative (yet market-based), short-term incentive plan, coupled with an attractive (non-equity based) long-term incentive (retention) plan. The newly hired CEO realizes that if he decides to "walk," he will be leaving a good bit of money "on the table."

By the way, the owner is currently looking at offering the CEO participation in a nonqualified deferred compensation program. This program will allow the new CEO to voluntarily defer annual earnings and let his earnings grow tax deferred. This plan would also offer the company some very attractive financial benefits. Executive deferral plans are covered in Chapter 12.

Let's now look at a second case that involves another privately owned company. Below are some considerations that made this case particularly interesting:

- The 100% owner informed his leadership team, cautiously and confidentially, of his interest in putting the company up for sale; he realized, of course, that executive retention would be critically important to any prospective buyer.

- *The team members expressed a willingness to remain with the organization, with the understanding that they would participate in a long-term compensation plan.*

- *The CEO (and his team members) realized that, because of existing environmental issues, the company might not be salable.*

- *Some of the team members realized that, if the company was to sell to a larger organization, their role might be duplicative, and, because of this, they would not be needed by the acquiring company.*

- *The owner had heard horror stories from companies who had granted real equity so this consideration was "off the table." However, he agreed to share a certain percentage of any net proceeds from the sale of the company with his executive team.*

- *The owner was concerned about being locked into granting certain payout percentages to each of his team members, realizing that the personal performance of his executive team members might fluctuate from year to year.*

In an effort to meet the divergent needs of the various stakeholders, we developed 2 distinct, but integrated, long-term compensation plans that were flexible enough to reward the desired performance and outcomes, without allowing the executives to "double dip" on these plans:

- *A 3-year long-term incentive plan (LTIP) providing an attractive cash reward linked to company and participant performance. Participants could qualify for a reward under this plan if the company met its' performance goals, but didn't sell before the end of this 3-year performance period. It addressed the needs of those individuals who, while skeptical about if and when the company might sell, were willing to remain with the company for the defined performance period.*

- *A more lucrative net proceeds plan whereby team members could receive a share of the net proceeds derived from a change of control for remaining up to and through the course of an ownership transition.*

To prevent the likelihood of "double dipping," we incorporated a provision that if the company sold, following the payout of the 3-year cash-based LTIP, then any proceeds from the LTIP would simply be subtracted from the more lucrative net proceeds plan.

As it turned out, the company was successfully sold before the end of the LTIP performance period. The executive participants were paid in accordance with the net proceeds plan provisions; some were asked to stay on with the new owner; others parted amicably with cash in hand.

As you can see, the question really isn't whether or not to give EQUITY, but whether to offer a long-term compensation program and, if so, in what form. That leads to the question: What is the purpose of long-term compensation?

The purpose of long-term compensation is to attract, retain, and build "ownership participation" among key executives while focusing them on performance factors that will drive long-term profitable growth, enterprise value, and shareholder return.

To help you in your thinking regarding long-term compensation, we have provided an overview of some of the more common types of long-term compensation plans.

Equity Based Plans

Restricted Stock—A plan where an executive is granted shares of stock that are subject to forfeiture unless certain conditions (restrictions) are met. These restrictions can either be time-based or performance-based. An example of a time-based restriction would be having to remain with the company for five years. An example of a performance-based restriction would be having stock linked to achieving a pre-determined, 3-year earnings-per-share (EPS) goal.

Performance-based shares are now the most widely utilized form of equity-based long-term compensation. Time-based shares continue to be utilized in certain circumstances, such as when a company may need to recruit a top-notch executive away from a competitor, with the departing executive leaving a good bit of money "on the table."

The advantage of restricted stock is that it turns executives into owners, thus aligning their interests with that of the owners. Restricted stock also encourages retention, since an executive would be forgoing the value if they left prior to the end of the restriction period. Performance-shares have gained the most traction lately, because in addition to the above-mentioned advantages, these shares also have the ability to strongly link pay to performance.

A disadvantage of restricted stock is that it dilutes existing shareholders by issuing additional shares for which no purchase price was paid. Time-based shares are also criticized as being "freebies" because they lack a pay-for-performance relationship, outside of share price. In private companies, equity-based plans are often discouraged because the process of valuing a private company can be burdensome and expensive. Additionally, granting equity means bringing in new business partners who will carry voting rights unless otherwise specified.

Restricted stock is expensed over the restriction period, at fair market value at the time of grant. The gain is taxed to the executive as ordinary income at the time of restriction lapse. The executive does have the option to make an IRC 83b election and pay taxes at the time of grant on what is presumably (or hopefully) a lesser value than at the time restrictions lapse.

Restricted Stock Units—A variation on restricted stock is "restricted stock units." Restricted stock units ("RSUs") are very similar to restricted stock but under this type of award, the actual shares of stock are not issued until the vesting date occurs and, in some cases, the company may have the discretion to distribute in kind or in cash equal in value to the shares at the time of vesting. Vesting may be time based or performance based and performance based

RSUs are often referred to as "performance shares" or "performance stock units" ("PSUs"). An RSU or PSU is treated as an equity grant taxable at the time of vesting and no IRC 83b election is available at the time of award. RSUs and PSUs are essentially the same as "phantom stock" but are payable in stock rather than cash. They are also more flexible than restricted stock grants in that they may be paid in cash or partially in cash to cover tax withholdings and the timing of the issuance of the shares may be deferred beyond the vesting date in order to defer taxes if structured appropriately.

Stock Options—A plan that grants an executive the right to purchase a fixed number of shares of company common stock at a fixed price over a specified period of time.

In the past, stock options were the most widely utilized form of long-term compensation, but their usage has been declining every year due to changes in accounting and tax treatment and lack of pay for performance relationship.

One advantage of utilizing stock options is that the design of these plans can be very flexible. Additionally, because executives must invest their personal money, they have a vested interest as owners.

One of the disadvantages is that options are taxed when exercised, so there is no tax deferral. This is burdensome for an executive who must have the money to both exercise the options and pay the taxes. Options have also been criticized for encouraging risky executive behavior in an effort to drive up stock prices with little regard for the downside. Options also have no linkage to performance outside of share price. In private companies, equity-based plans are often discouraged because valuing a private company can be a burdensome and expensive endeavor. Additionally, granting equity means bringing in new business partners who will carry voting rights unless otherwise specified.

Options are expensed over the vesting period, at fair market value at the time of grant. The gain is taxed to the executive as ordinary income at the time of exercise.

Most stock options (those described above) are considered nonqualified. An alternate variation, incentive stock options, has more plan design restrictions, but allows for capital gains tax treatment rather than ordinary income.

Phantom Equity Based Plans

Phantom Stock—These plans can be designed in a variety of ways to mirror the value of equity-based plans without the complications of using real equity. Rather than granting actual shares, awards represent a promise to pay the employee the equivalent cash value of the shares at some point in the future.

These plans are useful in situations where companies do not want, or cannot have, employees owning actual shares, but want to share equity-like value. Since these plans do not issue actual shares, shareholder equity is not diluted.

A disadvantage is that phantom stock plans, like equity plans, are linked to company value, which isn't necessarily the only indicator of company performance. However, performance measures could be incorporated into such a plan. These plans can also be more difficult to communicate to employees who are skeptical of a plan that doesn't grant them real equity.

One of the most popular versions of a phantom stock plan is what we have coined a "net proceeds plan." This type of plan only delivers its value to the executive(s) if a change of control occurs during their employment, which is, of course, the "big ticket" event for many private company owners.

Nonqualified Stock Alternative Plan—A flexible deferred compensation plan that, like a phantom stock plan, can be developed to mirror an equity-based plan but with several tax and other advantages to the organization and participants. The greatest advantage of the plan is that there is no company stock dilution for the current shareholders but provides participants with true secondary investments.

Cash Based Long-Term Plans

Performance Award (Long-Term Incentive Plan)— Performance awards are essentially incentive plans tied to performance of ≥1 year and designed to pay out over multiple years. Performance awards can be linked to a number of measures: improvement in share price; earnings before interest, tax, depreciation and amortization (EBITDA); sales; and quality.

Performance awards are becoming increasingly prevalent in both private and public companies. They can be utilized as a sole long-term plan or coupled with an equity (or phantom equity) plan.

These plans are advantageous because of their simplicity and the fact that they can directly link pay to performance. They are attractive because they are infinitely flexible in design and can be settled in cash. In addition, these plans do not dilute shareholder equity.

Performance awards are sometimes criticized because: (1) they do not provide executives with a true ownership stake, and (2) it is sometimes difficult to establish accurate long-term goals.

The estimated value of such plans should be accrued over the performance period. Any payout is taxable to the executive as ordinary income when vested and paid. Alternatively, payouts could be placed into a nonqualified deferral plan in order to offset the current tax implications.

Executive 162 "Stay" Bonus—A tax-advantaged plan that incents executive retention. The annual bonus amount is paid into a Tier One corporate-owned life insurance (COLI) policy. The employer has a great deal of flexibility in designing these plans and may tie bonuses to performance and/or the company's stock appreciation.

While the above list offers you a number of choices, there are others. The plan you select should address your unique circumstances. A careful analysis conducted by a skilled executive compensation consultant should help you to arrive at your optimal plan.

At this point you will want to begin to consider the following topics as you move forward:

1. **Eligibility.** Who are your key strategic leaders whom you need to retain and motivate to drive long-term performance and value?
2. **Payout "Multiples" (Targets).** What is a competitive long-term incentive target for the attainment of reasonable "stretch" performance? How does this fit in with your current offerings and total compensation strategy?
3. **Delivery Vehicles.** What makes the most sense for your particular scenario: equity, phantom equity, cash, etc.? Should you be confined to one vehicle or should you take a "portfolio" approach?
4. **Payout Metrics for Various Levels of Performance.** What will constitute threshold, target, and superior performance? What will be the "payouts" associated with such levels of performance?
5. **Performance Measurements (Goals).** Based on the plan you have chosen, to what will performance be tied? If utilizing multiple goals, how will they be weighted?
6. **Performance Period Length.** What constitutes a reasonable long-term horizon in your business? Keep in mind that, if the timeframe is too short, you're basically offering a second short-term incentive and doing little to retain your executives or drive long-term performance. However, if the horizon is too long, the incentive may lose some of its potency and fail to drive the desired performance and behavior. We find the most common performance period is 3–4 years.

7. **Frequency of New Plans.** Will plans be "rolling" such that a new plan begins each year and overlaps with earlier plans? Or will a new plan only begin once the previous cycle has been completed?

8. **Vesting.** Once the performance period has ended and the payout determined, will it be paid out all at once or vest over a period of time?

9. **Provisions.** What other provisions and contingencies must be addressed before developing all plan documents and communications?

Remember, your long-term incentive plan needs to be aligned with your company's strategic plan and associated goals. The plan needs to be designed carefully, as long-term compensation often represents the largest portion of an executive's total compensation "mix." While the company's short-term incentive plan may be a company's most potent vehicle for driving short-term performance and behavior, the long-term incentive plan may be the most potent vehicle for driving long-term performance and value, and retaining the key executives charged with doing so.

A well-designed long-term incentive plan should communicate:

- Where the company is going (vision)

- How it is going to get there (strategy/key initiatives)

- What it needs key people to do (roles, goals and expectations)

- How it will reward that effort (incentives)

Now, you may be thinking that this is all fine and well, but I'm not sure that I need to offer my executives a long-term plan, and maybe I don't want to. Again, there is nothing that says that, as a private company CEO or business owner, you need to offer such a plan. However, the job market has rebounded from our recent recession, and you may wish to ensure that your rewards program is still deemed to be competitive.

According to a May 2013 survey by OI Partners, 70% of the respondents stated that retaining talent was their greatest challenge. In fact, 51% of the surveyed companies indicated that they were experiencing greater turnover in 2013 across all organizational levels, and 75% are anticipating further turnover. Below are a couple of excerpts from this study:

- 34% indicate higher turnover among "high potentials"

- 29% stated that they had lost more senior level talent than the previous year

- 27% experienced higher turnover in the middle management ranks (Hollon, 2013)

Study participants were especially concerned about losing "high potentials" and mid-level managers who are viewed as the future leaders of their companies.

Bear in mind that offering a long-term compensation plan need not represent an expensive endeavor; in fact, the plan can be designed to be self-funded and should provide a solid return on investment (ROI).

When headhunters try to recruit some of your key executives, you may wish to make it more difficult for them to do so. If all they feel they have to do is offer a higher salary or bonus value, recruiting may not prove to be too difficult in today's market. But if your executives understand that they may indeed walk away from a good "chunk of change," it will make it more difficult for them to leave you.

Chapter 9

Selecting and Aligning Your Performance Goals

Over the years, many companies have made progress in their efforts to link pay to performance. In fact, a number of these have developed clear-cut performance metrics and associated payout formulas. These efforts have helped them to achieve a better return on investment (ROI) from their executive compensation programs.

Despite these advances, we have found that most companies suffer from the same weakness: the inability to properly select and align the right goals throughout the organization. Interestingly, many of these same organizations have taken pain-staking efforts to ensure that their employees understand how to write SMART goals; that is, goals that are Specific, Measurable, Action-Oriented, Realistic and Time Sensitive. Most of the C-level executives we have worked with struggle in selecting the right top-level organizational goals. Of course, if senior management doesn't select the proper goals at the top of the organization and ensure that these goals are compatible, conflicts will materialize, motivation will suffer, and the company will fail to achieve the desired synergy and results. This, quite frankly, has been the reason so many management by objectives (MBO) programs have failed and gone by the wayside.

While many of our clients have asked us to teach their managers and employees how to properly articulate their performance goals, more and more have invited us to provide training on selecting the right goals. These latter efforts have been extremely well received with proven short- and long-term results.

As we've searched for and tried to share best practices, we have found that a significant and growing number of leading companies are extremely goal-oriented. They have also become quite skilled at selecting and articulating the right top-tier goals and then aligning them up, down, and across their organizations.

Many leaders of less successful organizations think about goals just as often, but fail in their efforts to create a synergistic, goal-based culture. Since this topic is so important, we've provided the table on the next page to guide you in your efforts.

When you decide to implement or update your organization's incentive program(s), don't forget effective goal setting. Selecting, articulating, and aligning the right goals will allow your organization to achieve the greatest return on investment from its incentive plans.

Selecting and Aligning Your Performance Goals

Criteria	Less Effective Organizations	More Effective Organizations
Number of Top-Tier Goals	Too few or too many goals	5 – 7 clear cut goals
Balance	Top-tier goals are strictly financial	Goals are balanced (include both financial and non-financial criteria)
Clarity	Goals are "fuzzy" (hard to measure/ ensure the proper focus for both team and individual efforts)	Goals are SMART (specific, measurable, action-oriented, realistic and time-sensitive)
Compatibility Between Departments	Department goals conflict with one another (e.g. sales vs. operations)	Goals are carefully established to create win-win scenarios across department lines
Engagement/ Ownership	Employees are given "their" goals	Employees draft personal goals after reviewing those of their supervisors
Alignment	Goals are poorly aligned and ineffective	Each employee's goals support higher level supervisory/organizational goals
Communication	Goals are formally discussed 1-2 times per year; yet real accomplishments are hard to assess at year-end	Employees brief supervisors on goal progress on a regular basis; supervisors become coaches in helping their employees to succeed
Motivation	Goals process breaks down; initiative becomes another "program of the month"	Employees become engaged, proactive and flexible; goal focus spills over into other areas of their lives
Long-Term Effectiveness	Supervisors/employees resort to old habits	First year results tend to be good; results improve each year as new habits are ingrained

Chapter 10

Getting Even More From Your Incentive Plans

One of our favorite stories deals with one of America's most successful companies. What makes this story particularly intriguing is that the company almost went bankrupt!

Back in the early 80s, Springfield Remanufacturing Company (SRC) spun off from International Harvester. SRC remanufactures heavy-duty engines; a very messy business. The company was failing and employee morale had taken a toll. Most of the employees didn't feel too good about management and the feelings seemed mutual.

Nearing the brink of disaster, SRC's Chief Executive, Jack Stack, brought the troops together and offered them the following deal: He would teach them the business and, if they could turn things around, they'd all share in the management bonus.

What happened was nothing short of a miracle. Not only did the company survive, but became an American icon. The company's revenue climbed from $16M to over $400M and the stock price soared from 10 cents to $134 per share—that's right—from 10 cents to $134 per share!!! And during this time, SRC has spun off 17 companies (Wikipedia).

Jack knew that the purpose of the business was to generate cash for the owners, and if the employees were to ever think like owners, they needed to understand the business, including the numbers behind the business. Jack was credited with coining the term "open book management," which involves sharing company financials with employees. He also began preaching about the importance of business education. Open book management immediately began drawing the attention of the media and the company began holding onsite conferences and sharing their approach to open book management with other forward-thinking companies. LTC Owners Terry and Larry Comp were among thousands of business executives and owners who traveled to SRC. During their respective trips, Terry and Larry had an opportunity to meet hourly employees who had risen through the ranks and been given the opportunity to run some of the company's "spin offs." Terry developed a passion for teaching employees business fundamentals and became one of the recognized pioneers within the field of "business literacy."

You may be wondering why we began this chapter with this story. Well, one day as we were looking back at the many opportunities we've had to help our clients in developing their incentive compensation plans, we came to a starting realization: our greatest success stories had one thing in common—a secret success ingredient. It was, that in each of these client engagements, we had been asked to first teach their employees the basics of business, including their own business.

Getting Even More From Your Incentive Plans

Here's an important fact that we've learned—many employees are hungry for this type of information. At their core, most are looking for an opportunity to make a difference—to make their contribution. Below is one of our case studies that illustrates how business training can engage and motivate the troops while making a big difference to the bottom line.

Several years ago we were chatting with the CEO of a $25M (revenue) services company. During our conversation, he expressed frustration with the lack of employee engagement and the sense of entitlement he felt permeated his organization. The CEO had ambitious goals for his company, but it was just "humming" along. He had recently learned about the benefits of teaching business essentials to employees and knew that one of our partners was a pioneer in the area of open book management and teaching the essentials of business.

Soon, the CEO invited us to teach business fundamentals to his employees with a specific focus on THEIR business. In no time, it became apparent that they were hungry for this type of training and soon began to "connect the dots." It was great to witness morale improving as well as the business gaining traction.

Unfortunately, bad things happen. The company lost its biggest client, which accounted for roughly one-third of its business. Immediately, the executive team began meeting behind closed doors (in an effort to keep the news quiet), while they figured out how to solve the problem. Budgets were immediately cut to the bone. Shortly thereafter, employee morale and trust levels sank to a new low.

When we followed up with the CEO, we asked if he had involved the troops in identifying cost savings. (After all, they had just completed a series of business classes and might be able to help.) To make a long story short, he strongly doubted whether the employees would be able to do so, but agreed to let us design a 60-day "Gainsharing" Program. As part of this initiative, the employees were asked to nominate a team of their peers who would review cost savings suggestions and determine which were legitimate. To add some flavor to the program, we asked the employees to come up with a theme, which they did: Show Me the Money!

Prior to the launch, the CEO reiterated that his management team had racked their brains and insisted there were NO more cost savings to be found. Yet, within a matter of weeks, the employees of this small private company uncovered over $300,000 in "hidden" savings! Perhaps none of us should have been surprised. After all, the employees were closest to the customers, had been trained to better understand their business, and had a chance to show off their stuff.

Soon afterward, we got a call from the company's HR Director informing us that the CEO was walking around "like Santa Claus," delivering "Gainsharing" checks. In retrospect, the money seemed far less important to the employees than the pride they realized from helping their company get back on track.

We all know that money has the power to motivate and you may be thinking that money may have been a significant factor in this story. So let's take a look at another case study:

A local manufacturing company had also become intrigued with the concept of open book management and teaching business essentials. They invited us to teach a series of short business classes to their management and professional staff. The training was a big hit and we were subsequently invited to roll out the same type of training to their production folks. This group was even more fun to teach and it was gratifying to see the light bulbs come on.

Immediately after the training, the company's chair invited us to help the company tackle its biggest problem: on-time delivery. When we asked him what the OTD percentage was, the chair's face turned beet red. He admitted that the company had no idea, and then mentioned that he would be eternally grateful if we could: (1) help them identify their true metrics, and (2) provide them with an understanding of how to improve OTD performance, as this problem was causing them to lose some of their biggest clients.

To make a long story short, we found out that their OTD was 77%, meaning that 23% of the time their clients weren't receiving their shipments on time. We ended up facilitating a few meetings with a small cross section of the new "business essentials" graduates. Within 2 months, OTD climbed from 77% to 94%—and by the end of the year, reached 98%—we were excited to see the troops turn the company's biggest weakness into its most significant strength—all within a matter of a few months.

Oh yes, there was no monetary incentive tied to this critical business initiative.

It's not difficult to understand why business essentials training is such a potent tool. We ask employees to set goals and we tend to be disappointed with the outcome. It's no wonder—if they don't understand the business, how can they know what the key problems are, and where to focus their energies?

Taking some time to teach employees the basics of your business conveys a level of respect and sends a message that "we're all in this together and we need your help."

When you're looking to get an even bigger "bang-for-the-buck" on your short- and long-term incentive plans, consider carving out a bit of time to help your employees to help you.

Chapter 11

Managing Performance

Student: "Teacher, how would you define the state of performance appraisal in today's organization?"

Teacher: "That human encounter which keeps the manager awake the night before and the employee the night after."

Wow—while the above dialog is meant to be humorous, it creates quite a picture!

When I (Larry) got my first corporate job, I recall doing some extensive research on performance appraisal. The findings were quite controversial, but largely disappointing. Now, some 30+ years later, it seems that not much has changed. Sure, we now have software packages that allow us to fill out our appraisal forms online, and some more current approaches, such as 2-way and 360-degree feedback, but it doesn't feel like we've come very far.

We all have our own performance appraisal stories—some good, some not so good. I'll share a couple of my own to add some flavor. Early on in my career, I worked for a prestigious global automotive distribution company. Our Vice President of Human Resources was a really big guy and quite intimidating. Legend had it that he had once negotiated with Jimmy Hoffa, the high-profile criminal and head of the

International Teamsters Union. Once I was promoted to Manager of Human Resources Planning and Development, I ended up reporting directly to the VPHR. The morning of the day I was scheduled for my performance appraisal, my prior boss pulled me aside and gave me some advice. He suggested that I just let the VPHR "give me" my appraisal rather than entering into any dialog. I followed his advice and got through the appraisal process (which was largely positive), unscathed. However, I have to admit that the process certainly wasn't engaging—or motivating.

I received my last appraisal during my final corporate stint, which was with a global medical device leader. Prior to the appraisal discussion, I was asked to complete and forward my copy of the appraisal form—about two weeks in advance. My supervisor said he would also complete his copy in advance. Now this appraisal proved to be a much different experience. It became immediately clear that my boss had taken a good bit of time to read and think through my comments. And, while he didn't necessarily agree with everything I said, he encouraged dialog and handled the appraisal like a pro. He was well-prepared, relaxed, objective, and thorough. In fact, he identified and complimented me on some key accomplishments I had neglected to mention. Not only did I feel engaged during the process and motivated following our discussion, I found that our relationship had risen to a whole new level. I'm happy to say that, once we both left the company, we became good friends and continued our relationship.

What does this have to do with executive compensation? Well, can you really have a good executive pay for performance compensation program without a good performance appraisal system? Also, do senior executives do a better job facilitating this process than lower level managers and supervisors? Actually, in many organizations, it's the CEO or business owner who fails to get his or her appraisals done. That being the case, why should his/her reports feel compelled to take the appropriate time to effectively appraise their employees?

Performance Development vs. Appraisal

Over the last few years, more and more organizations have gravitated toward progressive approaches to the performance appraisal process. They have found these approaches to be one of their secrets to successful growth and employee engagement. In fact, an American Management Association study of 437 publicly traded companies found that the 205 organizations that utilized more progressive performance development practices demonstrated the following results:

- Increased profits, better cash flow, stronger stock market performance
- Significant gains in financial performance and productivity
- Significant sales growth per employee
- Lower real growth in numbers of employees

The chart on the next page illustrates some of the important differences between traditional per-

Traditional Performance Appraisal	Progressive Performance Development
Purpose and benefits unclear	Purpose and benefits understood at all levels
Process not supported by management	Leaders support and hold each other accountable
System lacks alignment/ integration	System linked to strategic direction
Appraisal focuses on past	Appraisal focuses on future
Process is too rigid	Process is flexible/ adaptable to changing circumstances
Supervisors lack training	All employees trained on purpose and workings
Process is administratively complex	Process is administratively simple
Process is viewed as an "event"	Process is an ongoing system of 2-way communication
Appraisals not conducted on time	Appraisals held in timely, comfortable manner
Process is exercise in conflict avoidance	Process entails leaders coaching for success
Employees surprised by feedback	No surprises!
Program yields a poor return on investment	Program yields a strong return on investment

formance appraisal and the more progressive approaches to performance development. Progressive approaches to performance development, while holding people accountable, recognize and attempt to address the following employee needs: (1) a clear sense of direction; (2) an opportunity to participate in setting goals and clarifying expectations; (3) timely, honest, and meaningful feedback on their performance; (4) consistency on how they are treated compared to others; and (5) support in achieving their goals.

To get the best results from your performance development process, keep these "top ten" principles in mind:

1. Integrate/align process with the desired organizational culture.

2. Demonstrate management support for the program.
3. Shift from a past, behavioral to a future, goal-oriented perspective.
4. Align goals horizontally as well as vertically throughout the organization.
5. Help employees to understand your business; involve them in the goal-setting process.
6. Streamline administrative aspects for optimal effectiveness/efficiency.
7. Determine how to appropriately link pay to performance.
8. Incorporate ongoing feedback to ensure there are no surprises.
9. Train managers on their respective roles and accountabilities.
10. Recognize that positive culture doesn't happen overnight: walk before you run.

Building a progressive performance development system around these 10 principles should help you and your staff in achieving a strong pay-for-performance compensation program. It should also help you and your team to get a good night's sleep, even during review season.

Chapter 12

Helping Your Executives to Build Capital for the Future

About 5 years ago, we received an urgent call from a close professional colleague, the Vice President of Human Resources for a local hi-tech company. He asked if I (Larry) could meet with he and his CFO as soon as possible. The next day we met for lunch and the two executives explained their dilemma. Their company had implemented an ineffective long-term capital accumulation plan that had totally "bombed." The problem, they explained, was that nobody understood the plan. And, of course, if nobody understands the plan, then it can't serve as an effective motivational or retention tool. To top it off, the company's CEO was on a rampage and wanted this problem dealt with immediately!

Fortunately, we were able to get our Executive Benefits partner, Bob Nienaber (who had designed our own company's executive deferral plan and had worked on thousands of other plans), to fly in and examine the plan with us. After facilitating a brief educational overview of plan considerations and design alternatives, Bob uncovered a number of deficiencies in the existing plan. He then provided a simple roadmap to solving our colleagues' problem. Bob was then asked to begin working with us to draft a non-qualified deferred compensation (NQDC) plan that was customized to the needs of the *executive participants, as well as the company. To make a long story short, the plan was subsequently approved and became a big "hit." Since then, the NQDC plan has expanded from 4 to over 35 participants and grown to more than $20M in assets. It has been extremely well received and has served as an exceptional tool for attracting and retaining executive talent while allowing them to build serious capital for the future.*

You may find that an executive deferral plan offers some significant advantages to your key executives while also helping you to build your balance sheet. Let's first zero in on nonqualified deferred compensation (NQDC) as a plan design alternative.

Nonqualified deferred compensation programs are not subject to the same set of ERISA laws governing qualified plans, such as 401(k) plans. NQDCs are not appropriate for each and every private company. However they offer several distinct and attractive features, such as:

- Plans may be limited to top management and are not subject to discrimination rules like qualified plans

- Eligible participants can defer whatever percentage of income (salary, bonus, long-term compensation) the company allows

- Plans reduce participants' current taxable income

- Executives defer current taxes while compounding tax-deferred earnings

- Investment choices can mirror those provided in a 401(k) Plan

Helping Your Executives to Build Capital

- Participants can set up special "in-service" accounts which allow them to take monetary distributions early without penalty

- Participants don't pay income tax until they receive distributions from their deferred compensation plan

- Companies can choose from among several funding vehicles

- Plans allow the company to build an asset, thereby strengthening its balance sheet

- Plans can be designed to parallel a company's time horizon (i.e., planned change of control) and pay-for-performance philosophy

- Plans are inexpensive to administer and can be structured to provide cost recovery

- Emergency distributions may be possible in the case of certain types of unforeseen financial hardships

- Plans can serve as an exceptional recruitment and retention vehicle—remember, a company's greatest expense is its investment in top people. Top companies use these plans to recruit and retain top talent

However, there are some additional factors to consider:

- Participant balances are subject to the claims of creditors of the corporation in the event of bankruptcy

- The corporation forgoes the immediate tax deduction on the deferred compensation, but will typically have a much larger deduction later when benefits are paid

A note of caution at this point: while there is no shortage of qualified plan (i.e., 401k) providers, there are relatively few non-qualified plan providers who understand the intimate details surrounding NQDC plans. This makes it difficult for most of us to be able to objectively evaluate alternative plan designs, product providers, and plan administrators.

Our executive benefits partner realized the above dilemma. A few years after we introduced him to the client mentioned above, he went on to co-create something that had never existed in the marketplace—a patented software program that examines over 200 points of differentiation to help interested companies objectively select the optimal product design, provider, and plan administrator. Over the last few years, many of our clients have utilized this tool and expressed their appreciation for its ability to help them to make the right decisions.

Special Considerations for "S" Corporations

The above case study pertains to a public company client of ours. NQDC plans are very beneficial to many "C" corporations, as well as many "S" corporations. While we were first working with the public company cited above, our practice had about a dozen employees, and was operating as a "C" corporation. A few years later, the 3 partners realized that their goals were no longer in parallel and decided to part ways. Two of the partners, Larry and Terry, formed LTC Performance Strategies, Inc. Our firm's CPA advised, under our new parameters, that we transition from a "C" to an "S" corporation. That all sounded good, but we were a bit concerned about our ability, going forward, to be able to defer enough money to meet our long-term capital accumulation goals. However, once we started working more closely with our CPA and the actuary he recommended, we learned that, as an "S" corporation, we still had the opportunity to defer large sums of monies as we were (financially) able to do so.

Our financial team showed us that we could integrate our 401(k) plan with a profit sharing plan. Because of the demographics associated with our now "slimmed down" organization, the 2 partners could each "sock away" about $50,000 per year ($100,000 total) under the integrated plan.

Our actuary also talked with us about setting up a defined benefit plan (pension plan). While initially skeptical, we listened closely. Here's a bit of what we learned: These plans promise to pay eligible employees specified monthly benefits at retirement. Such plans are formula-driven and may be based upon factors such as salary and service. These plans are tax deductible to the employer and tax-deferred for the participating employees. Depending upon many variables, these plans could provide attractive benefits for our employees and significant capital accumulation for the owners.

Let's look at some of the advantages and disadvantages of a defined benefit plan:

Advantages

- The plan provides a predictable benefit, and benefit accumulations can exceed $2M.

- The plan is tax-deductible for the employer and tax-deferred for employees until retirement distributions are made. Employers can contribute more into a defined benefit plan than other qualified plans.

- Any business entity of any size can sponsor one of these plans. These plans can be combined with other qualified plans, like 401(k)/profit sharing plans. The employer can establish eligibility and vesting requirements. The plan can utilize a wide variety of investment choices.

Disadvantages

- Annual contributions are required; under certain conditions the plan may be "frozen"; otherwise, an excise tax may be applied if the minimum annual funding requirement is not met.

- Participant assets are pooled, so there are no individual directed accounts. The employer bears the investment risk/reward.

In short, what we're saying is, as an "S" corporation (like so many private companies), we have benefitted from having the 401(k)/profit sharing, as well as the pension plan. Each year, we work closely with our CPA and actuary to ensure these plans are properly funded. The plans have helped our existing employees to save a good bit for retirement and have provided significant tax-advantaged capital accumulation for our partners.

Whether you are a "C" corporation, an "S" or "LLC," know that there are plans available to benefit the owners as well as the employees. Each organization, however, has its own unique characteristics, including demographics, and should seek proper guidance from its advisors.

We only wish we would have taken advantage of these plans earlier.

Chapter 13

Remaining in Compliance

A few years ago, a local attorney, seeking an expert witness, contacted us for a case he was building. The case involved a family-owned C corporation, in which the CEO was the majority owner, and his non-employee sister was the minority shareholder. The sister had filed a lawsuit against her brother, alleging that he was paying himself an unreasonably large salary and annual bonus.

We quickly learned that there was no love lost between the brother and sister.

You see, in a C corporation annual wages are not double-taxed like dividends. So each year, the CEO would pay himself a huge salary, and then bonus himself all (or most) of the company's net income. In doing so, this left little to nothing in dividends to split with his sister.

All of our due diligence in researching this case pointed to one thing: the CEO was unreasonably overcompensated. As such, he was not only "ripping off" his sister, but also the IRS! Once the details surrounding this case became more vivid to the attorneys on both sides, the case was quickly settled.

Owners of private companies need to exercise care in how they pay themselves. In essence, payouts of salaries, as well as any bonuses or dividends, need to be structured in such a way as to not "shortchange" the government. Please note, however, that what is considered "unreasonable compensation" depends upon whether the company is a C corporation or an S corporation. Also, at the time of this printing, the IRS does not have a uniform set of guidelines for determining reasonable compensation.

In a C corporation, wages paid are deductible by the company and taxed to the employee. However, shareholder dividends are not deductible by the company and are taxed to the employee; therefore they are double taxed. So when the "employee" is also an owner of the company, he/she may be inclined to take as high a salary and bonus as possible to avoid taking any dividends, resulting in the most advantageous personal tax situation. Since this results in less tax paid to the government, the IRS does not look favorably upon this and can actively challenge any salaries or bonuses they believe to be UNREASONABLY high.

S-corporations are pass through entities: all net income ends up being claimed by the owner(s) of the organization and not the organization itself. When an employee is also an owner of the company, he/she may be inclined to take as low a salary as possible to avoid payroll taxes and take the money as a shareholder distribution instead. Since this, again, results in less taxes being paid, it puts the owner at risk of an IRS audit.

Although the "flags" of unreasonable executive compensation are completely opposite for S and C corporations, the solution to the issue is the same. Owners/executives of private companies should do their due diligence in establishing their salaries.

These should be within a comparable range of relevant compensation survey market data. Likewise, any bonuses should be reasonable and linked to company performance.

We realize that many private company owners have very aggressive growth goals, which may include "going public"—good for you! Bear in mind, however, that this is an expensive process and doing so will result in your company having to comply with stringent Dodd-Frank legislation and intense scrutiny from proxy advisors: Glass-Lewis and Institutional Shareholder Services (ISS). Additional details will follow in our next book that addresses executive compensation in public companies.

Chapter 14

For Business Owners Only

A school supply business was generating slightly over $1M in annual profit. A larger competitor approached the business owner with a proposition to buy his business. While the proposition was tempting, the owner wasn't sure he was ready to sell. After seeking guidance from a recommended specialist, the owner set out on a course to drive up the value of the business to maximize his future options.

The specialist recommended specific actions to protect and enhance the value of the business and, over time, monitored a series of operational improvements that significantly improved the company's performance and value. A few years later, when his industry was consolidating, he was approached by a large national public company and the owner and his business were prepared. He consummated a sale and realized over $14M in cash.

At some point in time, perhaps soon, you will be looking to transition the ownership of your business. This transition could be precipitated by many factors: retirement, a seemingly attractive offer from a third party, or the decision to turn the business over to a family member.

Unfortunately, in the vast majority of these transitions, the owner fails to realize his/her financial or personal objectives. This is troubling, in that many of these owners have put their "guts" into their businesses and could have realized significantly better outcomes if they had just taken some time to prepare for the inevitable.

Transitioning to either succession or sale is one of the most significant events a business owner will face during his/her career. Yet, the vast majority of owners fail to plan and, as such, plan to fail. Previous business owners give all sorts of reasons why they didn't take the time to plan: 1) too busy with day-to-day matters, 2) expected a family member to step in, 3) didn't acknowledge the inevitability of the need to transition early enough, and, 4) didn't anticipate losing a key member of the management team. The bottom line: They didn't get around to it!

While we maintain that planning for the inevitable is a must, we do not advocate that each business owner develop a highly structured exit strategy focusing on only one type of business transition. Life is far too complicated to accurately predict your personal needs, the needs of your family, and the state of financial markets at some (unknown) point of time in the future. Though a written document is not necessary, certain steps should be taken to ensure that your needs, as well as the needs of your family members, are taken into consideration.

Understand all of your potential options. As the owner of your business, "cashing in does not mean you have to sell out." In fact, a sale as an initial transition may prove to be your least desirable option. Seek out and speak with an impartial specialist who can provide you with advantages and disadvantages of various transition alternatives.

Build the true value of your business. Regardless of when you transition to either succession or a sale, it is vitally important to recognize and optimize the enterprise's true value. Today, investors look for far more than the "numbers." They will be interested in intangibles such as the strength of the management team, employee stability/capabilities, and your organizational culture. Understanding and focusing on your business's true value is vital to preparing for the successful transition.

Carve out some time to position yourself for various contingencies. The optimal time to transition, of course, is when all the stars "line up properly"—the value of your company, the financial market, etc. Since it is impractical to predict exactly when such a transition will take place, prepare for this eventuality—it may be here before you know it.

Chapter 15

What To Do Now?

"Intelligence is taking something complicated and making it simple."
—C.W. Ceram

The above quote is not only one of our favorites, but has been a guiding principle in how we have operated our business over the last few decades.

There is no shortage of executive compensation books on the market. However, many are 200-300+ pages long, too detailed and overly theoretical. We realize that, in your role as chief executive or business owner, you need to focus on finding the future and leading your company to higher and higher levels. We also realize that there isn't a "snowball's chance in hell" that you're going to sit down and read through one of these 200+ page books.

For this reason, we've created the LTC Book Series to help you grasp the big picture while getting a better sense of areas of vulnerability and opportunity. In this first book, we've made every effort to distill the complex world of private company executive compensation into its essential elements.

In serving over 300 leading organizations, we have yet to find one whose compensation program couldn't stand some improvement. By now you probably have a pretty good idea how you would like to apply what you have learned:

- Do you need to figure out how to compensate a new leader you wish to add to your team?

- Are you seeking an innovative, cost-effective means of retaining key talent?

- Has your payroll gotten out of hand and you need to better manage salary costs?

- Do you have an "entitlement" culture and need to do a better job of tying pay to performance?

- Are you struggling with whether or not to grant equity to a key player?

- Are you looking for more creative ways for you and your executive team to save for retirement?

- Or perhaps, you are just in need of a general check-up.

Running a successful enterprise can be exhilarating and we wish you good fortune.

Of course, we all realize that a little knowledge can be a dangerous thing. This is especially true in the world of executive compensation, which continues to evolve rapidly. For this reason, should you have any questions at any time, drop us an email or give us a call.

Larry Comp and Steve Smith
LTC Performance Strategies, Inc.
28001 Smyth Drive, Suite 103
Valencia, CA 91355 (661) 294-2929

lcomp@ltcperformance.com
ssmith@ltcperformance.com
www.ltcperformance.com

LTC Performance Strategies, Inc., is independently owned and operated. Securities, when offered, are offered through FAS Corp., an SEC registered broker-dealer and member of FINRA http://www.finra.org. FAS Corp is an affiliate of Financial Advisory Service, Inc.

Appendix A

Sample Philosophy and Objectives Statement

Executive Compensation Program Philosophy & Objectives

COMPENSATION POSITIONING PHILOSOPHY:
- We offer attractive "**total compensation**" opportunities for *significant* company and individual performance.

PROGRAM OBJECTIVES:
- **Attract** and **retain** top caliber, well-suited executives
- **Incent** the desired **Company/ Department/ Individual performance & behavior,** while ensuring a strong "**pay-for-performance**" relationship
- Consider **key variables** (e.g. organization's size, stage of evolution, geographical market) in designing optimal **Total Compensation Program**
- Be externally **competitive, internally equitable,** and **consistent** in administration
- Ensure organizational **roles** are **clear,** yet appropriately **flexible**
- Ensure **titles** reflect roles and are **positively perceived**
- Provide appropriate opportunities for **personal/ professional development** and meaningful contribution
- **Contain** rising **employee benefit costs** while providing a **wide array** of **highly perceived** offerings
- Provide **executive benefits** that offer **income protection, tax savings,** and **investment** vehicles, as appropriate
- **Comply** with applicable local, state and federal **legislation**
- Ensure the program is **flexible** to **adapt** to changing business and organizational circumstances
- Ensure the program is **simple** to **administer** and **easy** to **understand**
- Ensure the program is **cost effective** and provides a solid (**ROI**)

Appendix B

Sample Job Description

Job Description

Company: xyz Company
Position: President & COO
Location: Los Angeles, CA
Department: Executive
Reporting to: CEO
FLSA Status: Exempt

General Purpose
Responsible for the profitable revenue growth, and the effective, efficient and ethical operation of the company, in line with its mission, vision and values.

Responsibilities
Essential functions of the job are listed below. Other responsibilities may also be assigned. Please note that the essential functions may vary depending on department size, organizational structure and/or geographic location. Reasonable accommodations may be made to allow differently-abled individuals to perform the essential functions of the job.

- Provides strategic direction and oversight in guiding the organization in achieving its goals for profitable revenue growth, increased shareholder value/ liquidity, and long-term organizational health.
- Guides development of strategic planning process and annual business plan in line with the organization's long-term vision.
- Monitors economic and industry trends; identifies growth opportunities, as well as potential threats to the organization. Assesses the strengths and weaknesses of other companies (competitors and non-competitors) in architecting a path to dominate strategic sectors.
- Plans, develops, and implements strategies used to generate new sources of revenue and opportunities for increased profitability. Seeks out and develops mutually beneficial partnerships.
- Partners with CEO in identification and diligence of acquisition and merger opportunities. Plans and directs associated implementation activities.
- Reviews activity reports and financial statements in tracking progress toward short and longer-term goals and objectives; takes corrective actions as needed.
- Ensures that the appropriate systems, programs, policies, and procedures are in place and that the organization complies with relevant legal mandates.
- Oversees Company operations to insure efficiency, quality service, and cost-effective management of resources. Provides oversight of vendor selection processes and desired outcomes, and negotiates key contracts for the Company.

- Ensures that the organization has the appropriate structure and right number of properly trained staff to carry out the organization's mission.
- Evaluates management's performance for compliance with established policies and objectives, and contributions towards goal attainment.
- Develops effective leadership team and plans for succession at various levels. Serves as a role model to direct reports and coaches/ counsels effectively to build effective leadership throughout the organization.
- Ensures effective corporate communication across the organization, including a unified presentation of leadership, and transmission of key strategic initiatives and other pertinent messages.
- Builds fundraising network utilizing personal contacts and involvement in special events and foundation support.
- Represents Company at legislative sessions, committee meetings, and formal functions.
- Promotes Company through personal appearances at conferences and to local, regional, national and international constituencies.
- Presents Company performance reports at Annual Stockholder and Board of Directors meetings.
- Handles various other duties as delegated by CEO and BOD.
- Carries out all responsibilities in an honest, ethical and professional manner.

Supervisory Responsibilities

In accordance with applicable policies/procedures and Federal/State laws, may perform the following supervisory responsibilities: Interviewing, hiring orienting and training employees; planning, assigning, and directing work; coaching and appraising performance; rewarding and disciplining employees; addressing complaints and resolving problems.

Minimum Qualifications

The following are the minimum qualifications that an individual needs in order to successfully perform the duties and responsibilities of this position. Please note that the minimum qualifications may vary based upon the department size and/or geographic location.

Knowledge
- Equivalent of a Bachelors Degree and 15+ years progressively responsible, related background, including proven experience in comparable senior leadership roles
- Keen understanding of the industry, including the ability to assess the strengths and weaknesses of competitor organizations, recognize and seek out relevant opportunities, and implement processes for improved efficiency, service, profitability, and growth.
- PC skills

Sample Job Description

Skills/ Abilities
- Ability to think strategically, synthesize the most complex business/financial data and develop innovative solutions
- Excellent planning, organizing, negotiating and leadership/supervisory skills; ability to focus/ align organization around critical initiatives and facilitate progressive change
- Strong staffing, development and appraisal skills
- Entrepreneurial spirit and willingness to take prudent risks
- Excellent verbal, written and executive presentation skills
- Strong customer, quality and results orientation
- Ability to interact effectively at all levels and break down barriers across departments/ diverse cultures
- Ability to be an effective member of and lead the most complex project teams

Appendix C

Sample Mini-Job Profiles

JOB TITLE	MAJOR RESPONSIBILITIES	MINIMUM QUALIFICATIONS*
Chief Executive Officer	Responsible for providing strategic vision, shaping the organizational culture, guiding the profitable revenue growth, and facilitating the effective, efficient and ethical operation of the company, in line with its mission and organizational values. Plans, develops and implements long-term growth strategies used to generate new sources of revenue and opportunities for increased profitability. while sustaining positive cash flow. Ensures that the appropriate systems, programs, policies and procedures are in place and that the organization complies with relevant legal mandates	Equivalent of a Bachelors Degree and 15+ years progressively responsible, related background, including proven experience in comparable senior leadership roles. Ability to think strategically, synthesize the most complex business/ financial data and develop innovative solutions. Excellent planning, organizing, negotiating and leadership skills. Ability to focus and align the organization around critical initiatives and facilitate progressive change. Strong staffing, mentoring, development and appraisal capabilities, along with proven verbal, written and executive presentation skills. Strong entrepreneurial spirit and willingness to take prudent risks.
Director, Marketing and Communications	Responsible for the organization's marketing and communications strategy and implementation, including: Brand/ message integrity, website design and content, print and online advertising, video development and production, social networking, special events, online store products, quarterly newsletter, monthly e-blast and organizational-wide campaigns. Recommends directs and implements improved systems, policies, and materials for communication and marketing efforts. Selects, orients, trains and manages staff members as appropriate.	Equivalent of a Bachelors Degree and 7-10+ years progressively responsible, related experience. Proven, related Marketing and Communications track record in a progressive environment that has experienced dynamic change and evolution. Excellent planning, organizing, negotiating and leadership skills. Strong staffing, mentoring, development and appraisal capabilities, along with proven verbal, written and executive presentation skills.

101

Works Cited

Beek, M. (n.d.). The Real Cost of Hiring Average Performers.

Economic Research Institute. (2013, 3 1). Executive, Salary and Geographic Assessors .

Hollon, J. (2013, 5 23). Survey: Half of Companies Report Higher Turnover Than Last Year. TLNT .

Miller, S. (2012, 8 15). Unanimity on 2013 Salary Forecasts Holding Up. Society for Human Resource Management .

Natitional Institute of Standards and Technology. (2001, 8 27). Malcolm Baldrige National Quality Award 1995 Recipient Corning Telecommunications Products Division.

Petrecca, L., and Strauss, G. (2012, 5 15). CEOs stumble over ethics violations, mismanagement. USA Today .

Sturman, M. (2003). Evaluating the Utility of Performance-Based Pay.

Wikipedia. (n.d.). Springfield Remanufacturing.

WorldatWork. (2007). Private Company Incentive Pay Practices.

Hopefully this book has piqued your interest as to how you can leverage your largest investment in driving performance and value in your company. LTC Performance Strategies provides real solutions in a timely and cost effective manner. For more information, please visit our website or contact us:

www.ltcperformance.com

Larry Comp: lcomp@ltcperformance.com

Steve Smith: ssmith@ltcperformance.com

LTCperformance
strategies